MARSHES AND SWAMPS!

J.K. O'Sullivan
Illustrated by Tom Casteel

Titles in the **Explore Waterways** Set

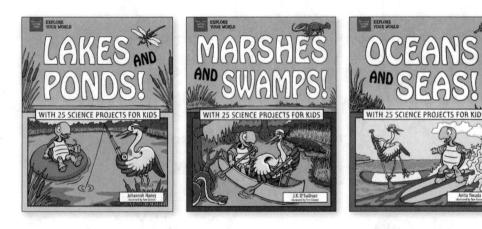
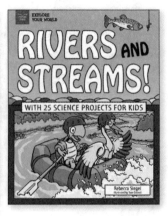

Check out more titles at www.nomadpress.net

Nomad Press
A division of Nomad Communications
10 9 8 7 6 5 4 3 2 1

This book was manufactured by Versa Press,
East Peoria, Illinois
November 2018, Job #J18-09188

ISBN Softcover: 978-1-61930-707-0
ISBN Hardcover: 978-1-61930-705-6

Educational Consultant, Marla Conn

Questions regarding the ordering of this book should be addressed to
Nomad Press
2456 Christian St.
White River Junction, VT 05001
www.nomadpress.net

CONTENTS

Interested in primary sources? Look for this icon. Use a smartphone or tablet app to scan the QR code and explore more! Photos are also primary sources because a photograph takes a picture at the moment something happens.

You can find a list of URLs on the Resources page. Try searching the internet with the Keyword Prompts to find other helpful sources.

→ **KEYWORD PROMPTS**

marshes and swamps 🔍

WHAT LIVES IN MARSHES AND SWAMPS?

Many plants and animals make their homes in marshes and swamps. Here is a glimpse of just a few—you'll meet many more in the pages of this book!

Only female **MOSQUITOS** suck blood! Males are fine with eating plants.

BULRUSHES are also called reed mace and corndog grass!

PAINTED TURTLES don't have teeth.

OPOSSUMS can eat about 4,000 ticks a week.
DEER TICKS aren't insects. They're classified as arachnids and related to spiders.
MUSKRATS can swim backward and forward.
Ancient Egyptians made papyrus out of a type of **SEDGE**.
SNAKES don't have eyelids!

INTRODUCTION

WHAT ARE MARSHES AND SWAMPS?

The places where land and water meet are very special. An amazing variety of animals make their homes there, while trees and grasses thrive. These places are more than simply beautiful and full of life. In some places, they are a link between land and water.

Land that is soaked with water for at least part of the year is called a wetland. Wetlands play an important part in keeping our environment healthy and are always changing. These are often important habitats for fish, plants, and wildlife.

WORDS TO KNOW

wetland: land that is soaked with water for part of the year, such as a marsh or swamp.

environment: a natural area with animals, plants, rocks, soil, and water.

habitat: the natural area where a plant or an animal lives.

1

Building roads and homes, filling in wetlands to turn them into farmland, and dumping waste are all activities that can destroy wetlands. When we lose wetlands, animals lose their habitats and their food sources. Our water quality suffers. That's why it's important to learn about wetlands. When you know more about wetlands, you'll know how you can help protect these amazing places.

MARSHES AND SWAMPS

Two of the most common types of wetlands are marshes and swamps. What's the difference between a marsh and a swamp?

Marshes are often found next to open water that's connected to other bodies of water, such as rivers or oceans. That means the amount of water in a marsh can change at different times of the day, in different types of weather, and in different seasons. As tides go in and out, the water level can rise and fall.

WHAT CAN YOU DO IN A WETLAND?

Wetlands play many important roles in the environment. But they are also beautiful places for people to enjoy. What can you do in a wetland? Try one of these activities: birdwatching, fishing, crabbing and oystering, canoeing, and kayaking.

Marshes can be fresh water, salt water, or brackish, which is a mix of fresh and salt water. Different types of grasses grow in marshes, but no trees grow there.

brackish: water that contains a mix of salt water and fresh water.

saturated: full of water.

hammock: an area of dry land rising out of a swamp.

WORDS TO KNOW

Swamps are areas where the soil is saturated. Here, the plant life is different. In swamps, woody types of plants, such as trees and shrubs, grow and thrive.

As with marshes, swamps can be fresh water, salt water, or brackish. Unlike marshes, some swamps have areas of dry land called "hammocks" that stick out of the water. These look like little hills in the flat swamp. Swamps are sometimes located near other bodies of water, such as rivers or lakes.

MARSHES AND SWAMPS!

RECOGNIZING A WETLAND

Imagine you are walking in the woods and you find an area of water on the ground. Maybe it's a puddle. Maybe it's a pond. Could it be a wetland? How do you know? Here are some questions you can ask to find out.

1. IS THERE STANDING WATER ON THE GROUND?

This can be a tricky question! Wetlands have standing water at some time during the year. But wetlands don't need to be wet all year round. Vernal pools are places where small, shallow pools are created in the spring or fall because of rainfall or snowmelt. These are wetlands that dry up for part of the year.

WHAT DO YOU GIVE A SICK ALLIGATOR?

Gatorade!

If you see a vernal pool or seasonal swamp in the summer, you might not recognize it at all! The soil may appear dry and cracked. But even then, vernal pools can provide food and shelter for animals through different plants that grow there.

2. WHAT KINDS OF PLANTS DO YOU SEE?

Certain types of vegetation grow in wetlands. In marshes, you will most commonly see grasses, sedges, cattails, and other flowering plants. In swamps, you might also see trees such as cypress, willow, red maple, and mangrove. These are trees that have shallow roots. If you see these trees, you are in a swamp, not a marsh.

soil: the top layer of the earth, in which plants grow.

vegetation: all the plant life in a particular area.

sedge: a grass-like plant. Many different sedges grow in wetlands.

mangrove: a tree or shrub that grows in tropical coastal swamps.

WORDS TO KNOW

CATTAILS

RUSHES

SPARTINA GRASS

CYPRESS

WILLOW

MANGROVE

MARSHES AND SWAMPS!

hydric: saturated with water for much of the year.

decompose: to rot or decay.

muck: muddy, wet soil.

peat: a substance formed from decomposing vegetation or other dead matter.

reptile: an animal covered with scales that moves on its belly or on short legs. It changes its body temperature by moving to warmer or cooler places. Snakes, turtles, and alligators are reptiles.

amphibian: an animal with moist skin that is born in water but lives on land. An amphibian changes its body temperature by moving to warmer or cooler places. Frogs, toads, newts, efts, and salamanders are amphibians.

WORDS TO KNOW

3. WHAT KINDS OF SOIL DO YOU SEE? The soil in wetlands is hydric. That means that it is saturated with water for much of the year. Often, the soil is made of decomposed plant material called muck or peat. Wetland soil is often a dark color and has a scent that some people think smells similar to rotten eggs!

4. WHAT ANIMALS DO YOU SEE? Wetlands are home to lots of different animals. You might see insects such as dragonflies and mosquitos. You might see reptiles such as snakes, turtles, and alligators, or amphibians such as toads, frogs, and salamanders.

6

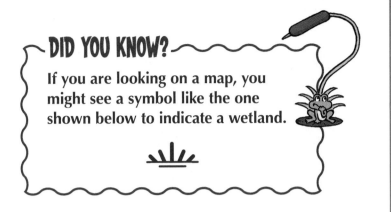

DID YOU KNOW?

If you are looking on a map, you might see a symbol like the one shown below to indicate a wetland.

mammal: a type of animal, such as a human, dog, or cat. Mammals are born live, feed milk to their young, and usually have hair or fur covering most of their skin.

debris: pieces of dead plants or branches.

bog: a wetland where plant material decomposes very slowly and builds up over time as peat.

carnivorous plant: a plant that traps and eats animals.

nutrients: substances in food and soil that living things need to live and grow.

WORDS to KNOW

You might also see mammals, large and small, from raccoons to moose to muskrats. Wetlands are full of life, but often the creatures that live here are hard to find. Be quiet and respectful and some of the marsh- and swamp-dwellers might come out to see you!

5. WHAT TYPE OF WATER DO YOU FIND?

Water in a wetland can be still or moving. It's usually a dark color. Often, there is debris, such as leaves or parts of plants, on its surface.

DIFFERENT TYPES OF WETLANDS

In this book, we are going to learn about marshes and swamps. But those are just two types of wetlands. Let's take a look at some of the others.

A bog is a type of wetland where the soil is made up mostly of dead plant material that is slow to decompose. Mosses are the main type of plants in bogs. Bogs are also home to carnivorous plants! These are plants that get their nutrients by trapping animals and insects because the undecomposed plant matter in the soil has so few nutrients.

MARSHES AND SWAMPS!

WORDS TO KNOW

evergreen: a plant that keeps its leaves or needles throughout the year.

fen: a wetland similar to a bog, except that it is fed by water from underground.

prey: an animal caught or hunted for food.

Evergreen shrubs can grow in bogs, too. You may have heard of cranberry bogs. These are places where the berries of a small evergreen shrub grow and are harvested in the fall. Bogs can be found along the coast, in high mountain meadows, and around lakes. A variety of birds and mammals can be found in and around bogs, including lemmings and moose.

A fen is similar to a bog. A fen differs from a bog by having an inlet and an outlet. A fen can turn into a bog as time passes, when vegetation blocks the inlet and outlet.

You can often find mosses in fens, and also grasses and sedges. Fens are habitats for insects, birds, and some mammals, depending on the climate—even beavers!

DID YOU KNOW?

Almost half the endangered animals in the United States depend on wetlands for habitat and food. These include the Florida panther, the whooping crane, and the red wolf. When we lose wetlands, our endangered animals lose an important source of food.

PS

Meet some carnivorous plants in this video!
Why are there so many different ways of catching **prey**?

KEYWORD PROMPTS

deadly carnivorous plants

biodiverse: full of many different types of life.

ecosystem: a community of living and nonliving things and their environment. Living things are plants, animals, and insects. Nonliving things are soil, rocks, and water.

species: a group of living things that are closely related and can produce young.

WORDS TO KNOW

TRUE OR FALSE

Learn more about wetlands with this True or False game!

The water level in a wetland is always the same.

False! A wetland only needs to be wet for part of the year. Sometimes, a wetland can be completely dry. The water level in a wetland usually increases during the winter and spring due to rainfall.

Most of the animals that live in swamps are dangerous.

False! Snakes, alligators, and mosquitos do live in swamps, but these animals are only dangerous under certain conditions. Many other harmless animals also live in swamps!

Marshes and swamps are full of quicksand.

False! The soil in marshes and swamps is often soft, but it's very rare for a person to get stuck in quicksand.

Marshes and swamps have been disappearing.

True! Many marshes and swamps have been drained or filled during the past 50 years to make room for houses and businesses.

Wetlands are the most biodiverse kinds of ecosystems.

True! Wetlands can contain hundreds of species of plants and animals.

aquatic: living or growing in water.

terrestrial: relating to the earth or non-saturated soil.

WORDS ⊚ KNOW

A mangrove forest can be found along a coastline. This is an area where trees called mangroves grow in brackish water. Mangrove forests are home to many kinds of birds and shellfish.

THIS IS WHAT IT LOOKS LIKE CANOEING THROUGH A MANGROVE FOREST!

Wetlands are an interesting mix. They have some of the qualities of aquatic habitats and some of the qualities of dry habitats, also known as terrestrial habitats. That's part of what makes them so special!

In this book, we'll learn more about the watery world of marshes and swamps. We'll meet lots of plants and animals that live there. We'll also discover the ways wetlands are useful to humans, and what we can do to protect these natural places.

Ready for a wet ride? Let's learn about marshes and swamps!

GOOD SCIENCE PRACTICES

Every good scientist keeps a science journal. Choose a notebook to use as your science journal. Write down your ideas, observations, and comparisons as you read this book.

For each project in this book, make and use a scientific method worksheet, like the one shown here. Scientists use the scientific method to keep their experiments organized. A scientific method worksheet will help you keep track of your observations and results.

Each chapter of this book begins with a question to help guide your exploration of lakes and ponds.

Scientific Method Worksheet
Question: What problem are we trying to solve?
Research: What information is already known?
Hypothesis/Prediction: What do I think the answer will be?
Equipment: What supplies do I need?
Method: What steps will I follow?
Results: What happened and why?

? INVESTIGATE!

What is the difference between a marsh and a swamp?

Keep the question in your mind as you read the chapter. Record your thoughts, questions, and observations in your science journal. At the end of each chapter, use your science journal to think of answers to the question. Does your answer change as you read the chapter?

PROJECT!

BE A WETLAND DETECTIVE

SUPPLIES

✳ local map (check your local library)
✳ science journal and pencil

Is there some kind of wetland near your home? Do you live near a river or lake? Or next to the ocean? Ask an adult to help you identify a local wetland to explore.

1 On your map, identify the nearest body of water. Is it a lake? Creek? Pond? River? Visit the place where you think you might find a wetland. What do you see, hear, and smell? Record your observations in your science journal.

2 If the area is dry, look at the bases of trees to see if you can find watermarks. Is the color on the bottom of the tree darker than it is farther up? That might mean that the base of the tree has been under water at some time.

3 Observe the different types of plants that are present. Make drawings in your science journal. Ask an adult to help you find a guide to wetland plants at the library or online to see if the plants here are typical wetland plants.

4 Do you see any animals, even small ones? Record your observations. Congratulations, you've become a wetland detective! Keep your notes and check them as you work through this book to determine if the places you visit are wetlands.

TRY THIS! Based on your observations, can you tell what kind of wetland this is? A bog, fen, marsh, or swamp? How do you know?

CHAPTER 1

WHY MARSHES AND SWAMPS MATTER

Wetlands have been called "nature's kidneys." That's because they serve some of the same functions as human kidneys, which are organs that filter the body's blood. Wetlands act as filters, just like kidneys do in your body, and they help keep the water clean. But that's just one of the important roles they play in the environment.

Wetlands are some of the most diverse ecosystems in the world. Not every wetland functions the same way, but let's look at some of the different ways wetlands help the environment.

? INVESTIGATE!

What role do wetlands play in our environment?

SHELTER AND FOOD IN WETLANDS

Wetlands provide habitat. Because water is so important to animals, they are drawn to marshes and swamps at all times of the year.

Small creatures such as insects lay their eggs in the water. Fish do, too. Worms burrow down in the soil. For birds, wetlands are a source of food. Migrating birds stop at marshes and swamps on their seasonal journeys. Amphibians like to spend the winter in water and wet soil. Even mammals live in marshes and swamps, because they can find food there, too.

The rich soil in wetlands provides many nutrients that help plants and animals thrive. Wetlands are part of the nutrient or nutrition cycle. In every wetland, plants, animals, and other organisms are part of this cycle as they grow, feed, die, and decompose. This creates an environment rich in nutrients. You will learn more about the nutrient cycle in the next chapter.

HOW DO CRABS MAKES PHONE CALLS?

On shell phones!

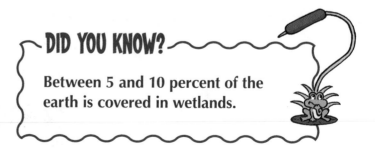

DID YOU KNOW?

Between 5 and 10 percent of the earth is covered in wetlands.

CYCLING AROUND

Have you heard of the water cycle? That's
the path that water takes from cloud to precipitation to the earth
and back up to the clouds. The nutrient cycle is the path a nutrient
takes from being eaten by an animal to being part of an animal
to being back in the ground. For example, imagine a worm eats a
decomposed leaf. Then, the worm is eaten by a bird. The bird makes
waste that falls onto the ground and goes into the soil. The soil helps
a plant grow to produce more leaves. Another worm eats one of
these leaves. It's the nutrient cycle!

BIRDS EAT THE WORMS, THEN MAKE WASTE.

WORMS EAT DECOMPOSED LEAVES.

WASTE FERTILIZES PLANTS, WHICH MAKE MORE LEAVES.

LEAVES FALL FROM THE PLANT AND DECOMPOSE.

flooding: when water covers an area that is usually dry.

absorb: to soak up.

excess: more than the normal amount.

groundwater: water that is held underground in the soil or in cracks and crevices in rocks.

drought: a long period of little or no rain.

carbon dioxide: a natural gas that's called a greenhouse gas. In excess, it contributes to the warming of the atmosphere.

climate change: a change in the long-term average weather patterns of a place.

atmosphere: the mixture of gases surrounding the earth.

WATER EVERYWHERE

Wetlands help prevent flooding. They absorb water, so they help store excess water during times of flooding. One acre of a wetland can store up to 1.5 million gallons of floodwater! That prevents that extra water from rising and flooding places where people live.

Marshes and swamps also help store groundwater. Because water stays in wetlands longer than other places, it can seep into the underground streams and pools that supply water to local communities. That's helpful in periods of drought.

WETLANDS AND CLIMATE CHANGE

Wetlands absorb and store carbon from the carbon dioxide gas that's in the air. That makes them important in the fight against climate change. Part of keeping the earth in balance is limiting the amount of carbon dioxide that is let into the atmosphere.

DID YOU KNOW?

Wetlands are like sponges, holding rain and snowmelt in wet seasons and releasing water in drier seasons, so there's less risk of floods and drought! How does this help the people who live in regions that flood?

When wetlands are destroyed, the carbon that they store is released. That's harmful to the atmosphere and to the earth's climate. We'll learn more about climate change in Chapter 4.

WETLANDS FILTER POLLUTION

A wetland is described as having a kidney function because it filters pollution. Chemicals, waste, and other pollutants can be carried by water as it moves from place to place.

This happens naturally when it rains because of something called runoff. Runoff is rain or snow or other precipitation that flows over the land and eventually reaches the lakes, seas, or other bodies of water.

climate: the average weather patterns in an area during a long period of time.

pollution: waste that harms the environment.

runoff: the water from precipitation that drains or flows over the ground into a body of water or a wetland.

WORDS TO KNOW

CELEBRATE WETLANDS!

February 2 is World Wetlands Day! It's a time to help raise awareness of the importance of wetlands around the world. Wetlands are very important in cities, suburbs, and the countryside. No matter where you live, your neighborhood is affected by wetland activity!

(PS) Find out how you can participate in a World Wetlands Day celebration at this website.

KEYWORD PROMPTS

World Wetlands Day 🔍

Runoff is full of sediment, or little pieces of soil. If the soil has been in the city, it might contain chemicals from cars or factories. If it comes from a farm, it might have chemicals such as fertilizers, that help plants grow. It might contain waste from the animals on the farm. All this waste and chemicals can end up in the water we use for drinking, bathing, and cooking.

When runoff reaches a marsh or swamp, it is slowed down by the plants that grow there. The plants also trap some of the solid waste so that it doesn't continue to spread with the water. The water that leaves a wetland is much cleaner than it was when it went in.

DID YOU KNOW?

Antarctica is the only continent with no wetlands!

When we lose wetlands, animals lose their homes and their food source. Our water quality suffers. That's why it's so important to know about and protect wetlands.

The animals that live in wetlands are a very diverse bunch of creatures! In the next chapter, we'll take a closer look at the plants that call wetlands home. These plants provide the food that feed the animals there.

? CONSIDER AND DISCUSS

It's time to consider and discuss: What role do wetlands play in our environment?

PROJECT!

MAKE A MODEL WETLAND

See for yourself how wetlands work by creating your own mini-wetland. Models are very useful when you want to see how something works!

1 Line the shallow part of your paint pan with a thin layer of modeling clay. Stop about two-thirds of the way down. This is your land. You can create little hills or rock formations on it if you like!

2 At the two-thirds point of the pan, lay pieces of sponge or floral foam across the width of the pan. This is your wetland area. Leave the last few inches of the deep end of your pan empty.

3 What do you think will happen if you spray or pour a large amount of water on the land in your model wetland? Start a scientific method worksheet to organize your experiment. What happens? Where does the water go? Record your observations.

4 Now, take out your wetland—your sponges—and spray or pour the water again. What happens? What's different? What does this tell you about how wetlands function and how they might help the ecosystem?

TRY THIS! Make your wetlands out of another type of material, such as felt, newspaper, cloth, sand, or something else. How does this change what happens to the water? Why?

19

PROJECT!

NATURE'S KIDNEYS

How do wetlands such as marshes and swamps filter pollution from water? Start a scientific method worksheet and try this experiment to find out.

SUPPLIES

* ✳ 2 measuring cups
* ✳ vegetable or olive oil
* ✳ potting soil or dirt
* ✳ water
* ✳ scissors
* ✳ plastic water bottle
* ✳ pea gravel or tiny rocks
* ✳ coffee filter
* ✳ plastic clips or big rubber band
* ✳ science journal and pencil

1 In a measuring cup, mix the oil, soil, and a little water. Set aside. Cut the bottom off the water bottle. Turn the top part upside down. Holding your hand over the opening, which is now at the bottom, place the pea gravel in the bottle.

2 Place the coffee filter below the bottle opening. Secure it in place with the rubber band or plastic clips. Position the water bottle inside the second measuring cup. Hold it up so it doesn't rest on the bottom of the measuring cup.

3 Pour the soil mix into the open part of the plastic bottle with the pea gravel. Then, pour in more water so it runs over and through the soil and gravel.

4 What do you notice about the water? Record your observations in your scientific method worksheet in your science journal.

THINK ABOUT IT! What do your observations tell you about how wetlands help filter water? Do you think every wetland filters water well? What might keep a wetland from acting as a good filter?

PROJECT!

GETTING GROUNDED

One of the functions of wetlands is to store groundwater. That's important because this water will be needed in case of drought or water shortages. How do marshes and swamps store groundwater? Start a scientific method worksheet and try this experiment to find out.

1 Pour a small amount of gravel or pebbles into the bottom of one jar—just enough to cover the bottom. Pour a thicker layer into the other jar.

2 Pour sand on top of the pebbles. In the jar with a thin layer of pebbles, pour more sand. In the jar with more pebbles, pour less sand.

3 Repeat this process for two additional layers of both pebbles and sand until the material reaches about 1 inch from the top of the jar. The last layer in both jars should be pebbles.

4 Pour water into the top of the first jar. Observe as the water flows down through the pebbles to the bottom. Repeat for the second jar. Continue pouring until you have standing water at the top of the jar. What did you notice about the way the water behaved when there was more sand? More pebbles?

THINK ABOUT IT! Did both jars take the same amount of water? What do you think that means for marshes and swamps? What do you think lies under the surface of the most absorbent marshes?

PROJECT!

SLIP SLIDING AWAY

Wetlands such as marshes and swamps help to fight erosion. **Start a scientific method worksheet and try this project to learn how erosion works and how wetlands work against it!**

> **Caution:** Ask an adult to help you cut the bottles.

1 Cut large windows into the sides of the soda bottles and cut the small water bottles in half widthwise.

2 Lay the soda bottles on a table with the open end facing up. Fill one with soil, one with soil and dead leaves, and the third with soil and grass, making sure to pat the grass roots down into the bottle.

3 Make the tops of the small water bottles into buckets. Have an adult help you use scissors to poke holes in the sides of the bottles and tie the twine to make handles.

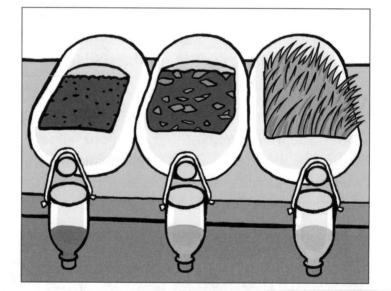

SUPPLIES

* 3 large plastic soda bottles with caps off
* 3 small plastic water bottles with caps on
* potting soil
* dead leaves
* grass (uprooted with soil still surrounding it)
* scissors
* twine
* pitcher
* water
* science journal and pencil

WORDS TO KNOW

erosion: the wearing away of a surface by wind, water, or other process.

4 Once you've got your buckets, hang one from the top of each larger soda bottle so that it sits just below the opening, as shown in the picture.

5 Slowly pour water into each of the soda bottles. After a few minutes, you should see water starting to run out of the bottle top into the buckets. What do you notice about the water? How does the water differ from container to container? Which water is cleanest? Record your observations in your scientific method worksheet in your science journal and draw pictures of your experiment.

TRY THIS! Repeat this experiment using different materials in the soda bottles. Which cleans water better, sand or large pebbles? A bundle of sticks or green leaves?

RUNOFF!

Wetlands can be polluted by storm-water runoff. Storm water is the water that is produced by heavy rain. When rain falls onto roads, parking lots, and other paved surfaces, it can't be absorbed into the ground. Instead, it travels over the surface and into drains, carrying pollutants with it. Have you ever seen the surface of a parking lot on a rainy day? What do you notice about it?

PROJECT!

OCEAN MOTION

SUPPLIES

* paint pan
* sand
* water
* measuring cup
* science journal and pencil
* plastic water bottle
* aquarium gravel

Have you ever been to a beach and seen grasses and other plants growing along the shore? Marshes can help prevent beach erosion. They do this by slowing down the force of the water from waves and absorbing the water as it flows into the marsh. To get an idea of how ocean waves can erode beaches and how dunes and marshes can help, start a scientific method worksheet and try this project. The dunes in this project will act as the first defense of the beach. The marshes or wetlands are the second "speed bump" for waves.

1 Fill the bottom of the pan with sand, with most of it in the shallow end. This is your beach.

2 For five minutes, slowly pour six cups of water into the deep end of the pan. How does the beach change as the pan fills? Where is the shoreline? Make a drawing of your beach in your science journal.

3 Place your plastic water bottle in the deep end of the water, submerging it. Roll it back and forth for a few minutes to create waves. How is the sand affected by the waves?

4 Empty your pan and create a new beach, this time with dunes. Make the dunes by pouring the aquarium gravel into little mounds at the shallow end of the pan. Cover these mounds with sand. These dunes should extend into the water a little.

WORDS TO KNOW

dune: a mound or ridge of sand that has been blown by the wind.

PROJECT!

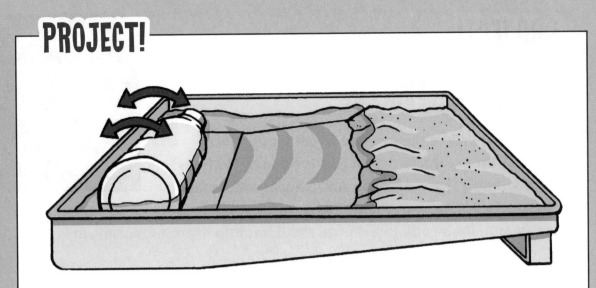

5 Repeat the process of slowly adding water to the pan and then making waves with the soda bottle. What happens to the dunes? What happens to the water? How is this different from your beach with no dunes? Write down your observations.

6 Finally, empty and refill your pan one more time. Make a beach and dunes again, but this time use the aquarium gravel to make a small wetland behind the dunes. Start this area with a layer of gravel and cover it with sand, but make it level, not raised like the dunes.

7 Repeat the process of making waves with the bottle. What happens now? Does the water enter your wetland? What happens when it gets there?

THINK ABOUT IT! Which type of beach was less damaged by the waves you made? Why? What does this tell you about the role of wetlands in preventing erosion?

MAKE A WATERSCOPE

You don't need a microscope to get an up-close look at the creatures that live in the water. With just a few simple items, you can make a waterscope at home. Take your waterscope to the nearest wetland or swamp for a good look at the small but important organisms in the water.

Caution: Only use with an adult present. Ask an adult to help you with the scissors.

1 Have an adult help you cut a circle out of the bottom of the plastic food container. Discard the center you cut out.

2 Cut the center out of the lid so that you just have the edge remaining. Discard the center you cut out.

3 Tear off a piece of plastic wrap big enough to cover the top of the food container and go about halfway down the sides. Stretch it over the top, then put the lid with no center back on the container to hold the plastic wrap in place.

PROJECT!

4 To use your waterscope, dip the plastic-covered end down into the water and look through the other end. It is helpful to be able to get partially into the water to do this if you can. If not, you can get close to the edge of the water without going in.

5 What do you see underwater? If you don't use your waterscope, what can you see?

THINK ABOUT IT! There are 5 million tiny **bacteria** per teaspoon in sea water. Imagine that!

FOCUS ON THE EVERGLADES

The Everglades National Park in southern Florida is made of 1.5 million acres of wetlands. As you might imagine, there are lots of plants, animals, insects, and amphibians living here! During the last couple of centuries, parts of the Everglades were drained or water was channeled to other areas so people could develop this land. However, efforts have been made more recently to conserve the Everglades. People recognize that these wetlands are critical for plant and animal species, and that the health of the entire region is better when the Everglades are kept whole and healthy.

You can watch videos about the Everglades at this website. Why are the Everglades so important?

KEYWORD PROMPTS

Everglades Nature Conservancy

CHAPTER 2

WILD, WEEDY, AND WATERY PLANT LIFE

Water is present in marshes and swamps for much of the year. That makes these areas perfect for plants to grow and thrive! In fact, in the United States, 31 percent of plant species live in wetlands. That's a lot!

Plants are very important to the ecosystems of marshes and swamps. When plants are alive, they provide both food and shelter for animals. After plants die and decompose, they provide food for other organisms and help to nourish the soil.

? INVESTIGATE!

In what ways are plants an important part of a wetland?

Many different plants grow in wetlands. Different plants depend on their watery or semi-watery environments in different ways. In turn, other plants and animals depend on them. Each species helps the wetland ecosystem thrive.

TYPES OF WETLANDS PLANTS

Three main types of plants grow in marshes and swamps. Let's take a look at them.

EMERGENT PLANTS: These plants grow on the edges of wetlands or in shallow water. They have roots that are usually underwater, while part of the plant extends out of the water. Examples of emergent plants include cattails, bulrushes, reeds, and sedges.

FLOATING-LEAF AND FREE-FLOATING PLANTS: Floating-leaf and free-floating plants live on the top of the water, and include water lilies, lotus, duckweed, and watermeal. Floating-leaved plants are rooted in the soil underwater and their leaves extend up to the water's surface. Free-floating plants really do just float on the water's surface.

SUBMERGED PLANTS: Submerged plants live completely under water. Examples include pondweed and eelgrass.

CREDIT: NOAA PHOTO ADAM OBAZA

In addition to these plants, some plants live entirely on dry land and some plants—such as mosses and lichen—even live on rocks.

LIKIN' THAT LICHEN!

Lichen are plants that are made of algae and fungi. Even though they don't have deep roots, lichen and moss can help stop erosion. They can also store carbon, a chemical found in the air. They help to filter pollution that can be found in rainwater. Lichen and moss provide a food source for many animals, even in times of drought. When lichen and moss decompose, they produce sediment that becomes soil.

Plants can root in this sediment and grow, even in rocky, barren places. Lichen and moss play an important role in the environment!

algae: a plant-like organism that turns light into energy. Algae does not have leaves or roots.

fungus: a plant-like living thing without leaves or flowers. It grows on plants and things that are rotting, such as old logs. Examples are mold, mildew, and mushrooms. Plural is fungi.

WORDS TO KNOW

THE NUTRIENT CYCLE

In marshes and swamps, plants are an important part of the nutrient cycle, which includes production, consumption, and decomposition. Let's look at these different parts of the nutrient cycle.

PRODUCERS → PRIMARY CONSUMERS → SECONDARY CONSUMERS

PRODUCTION: All living things use energy. Plants use carbon dioxide and energy from the sun to grow and thrive. They also use the nutrients they get from the water or soil. This is the production stage.

CONSUMPTION: Did you have salad for dinner or an apple for a snack? Living organisms, including humans, eat plants to get the energy they need to live. Some animals also get energy from eating other animals. This is the consumption stage.

DECOMPOSITION: When the life cycle of a living organism is over, it decomposes and becomes part of the soil. The nutrients in the decomposed material can then be consumed by another living organism. This is the decomposition stage!

Based on this cycle, living organisms in marshes and swamps are called producers, consumers, and decomposers. Producers make oxygen and their own food from sunlight, carbon dioxide, and water. In wetlands, plants are producers.

DECOMPOSERS

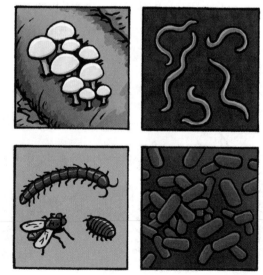

INVASIVE PLANTS

Invasive species are a problem in many wetlands. Some invasive species are animals and some are plants. Have you ever heard of Eurasian milfoil? Eurasian milfoil is an invasive plant that has been found in many bodies of water in North America. The plant is native to Europe, Asia, and North Africa, and likely was introduced to North American waters when people dumped aquarium water in lakes. The plants take up the nutrients and space that native plants need, crowding them out and taking over the entire body of water.

invasive species: a species that is not native to an ecosystem and that is harmful to the ecosystem in some way.

phytoplankton: tiny, drifting plants, such as algae, that live in both salt water and fresh water.

photosynthesis: the process plants use to turn sunlight, carbon dioxide, and water into food.

primary consumers: organisms that eat plants.

secondary consumers: organisms that eat primary consumers.

WORDS TO KNOW

Plants can be very tiny or quite large. Phytoplankton are the smallest producers. As with all plants, they use photosynthesis to produce food. Consumers, however, can't make their own food. They have to eat those organisms that do make their own food. In wetlands, there are primary consumers and secondary consumers.

DID YOU KNOW?

The largest organism in the world is an underground fungi in Oregon that measures more than 2 miles!

Primary consumers are organisms that eat plants directly and secondary consumers are those that eat something that ate the plant. If a bird eats a worm that ate some dead leaf material, which is the primary consumer and which is the secondary consumer?

33

organic: something that is or was living, such as animals, wood, grass, and insects. Also refers to food grown naturally, without chemicals.

invertebrate: an animal without a backbone.

zooplankton: tiny animals that drift freely in salt water and fresh water.

filterer: an animal that uses a filtering motion to feed. These animals include tiny animals such as krill and bigger animals such as whales.

WORDS TO KNOW

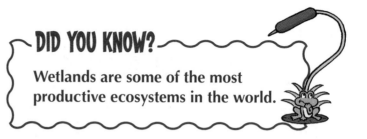

DID YOU KNOW?

Wetlands are some of the most productive ecosystems in the world.

Decomposers are often types of bacteria that break down other organic material, such as plants or animals. In wetlands, bacteria live in the water and consume dead plants.

Phytoplankton and those bacteria are eaten by invertebrates and zooplankton and even by bigger filterers, such as oysters and mussels. Then, birds and mammals, including raccoons, eat the oysters and mussels. Predators, such as alligators, might eat these animals.

HERE TODAY, GONE TOMORROW!

Vernal pools are one of the most interesting types of wetlands. These areas can fill and drain several times during a year, depending on the season and the amount of precipitation the area gets. Usually, a vernal pool is completely dry in the summer and fills up with rain, snow, and runoff during the other seasons. For several months out of the year, when they are filled with water, vernal pools are home to plants and animals.

(PS) **Meet some of the creatures that live in vernal pools in this video.**

KEYWORD PROMPTS

vernal pool video 🔍

When a creature dies, its body decomposes back into the soil. The body becomes a source of nutrients for the plants growing there and the cycle continues. This cycle of production, consumption, and decomposition is part of the food web in wetlands.

food web: the interconnected system of feeding relationships in an ecosystem.

indicator species: a species that can be studied to understand the overall health of an ecosystem.

salinity: the salt content of water or soil.

WORDS TO KNOW

HEALTHY PLANTS, HEALTHY ECOSYSTEM

Plants are good indicator species in wetlands. Scientists know the overall health of a marsh or swamp by measuring the health of its plants. Plants are sensitive to the soil, water, and air that are important to their growth.

If the water in a wetland is polluted or has too much salt in it, a plant's growth will be affected. If the air in a wetland is polluted, the plants won't grow well.

The same is true of the soil. If a wetland plant is damaged by pollution or salinity, those effects will be passed on to the consumers of the plant—the organisms that eat the plants.

If a plant species can't thrive in a wetland, the other organisms that live there might not be able to survive either. What does that mean for the overall health of the ecosystem?

In the next chapter, we'll learn more about the animals that depend on wetlands for food, shelter, and more!

? CONSIDER AND DISCUSS

It's time to consider and discuss: In what ways are plants an important part of a wetland?

PROJECT!

GROW YOUR OWN WATER PLANTS

Want to know how submerged plants grow? Try it for yourself!

1 Find an outdoor location for your pond. Try to find an area where the container will receive at least five hours of sunlight during the day.

2 Fill the bottom of the planter with about one-half inch of potting soil. Add a 1-inch layer of play sand on top of the soil. Plant your starter plants in the soil at the bottom and fill the pot with water.

3 If you are concerned about mosquitos laying eggs in the water, cover the container with some kind of screening or netting that you can get from a hardware or home improvement store.

4 In your science journal, make daily observations of your plants. What size are they? What is the water like? Is anything else growing in there?

WHAT KIND OF SHOES DO FROGS WEAR?

Open toad!

5 After about a week, you should notice the water turning cloudy, algae growing, and your plants growing. Observe how many more plants you have than when you started. What do you notice about the water? What do you notice about the way the plants grow?

6 When you are done with your experiment, dump your aquarium out on dry land, NOT in a stream, pond, or other body of water. Thank you for helping to keep wetlands healthy!

TRY THIS! How long can you keep your pond going? See how it lasts throughout the seasons where you live!

PROJECT!

GET GROWING!

The nutrient cycle plays out in marshes and swamps every day as plants and animals grow and decompose. Make your own mini-nutrient cycle in a bottle to get an idea how the process works in wetlands.

SUPPLIES

* 2-liter soda bottle with the cap
* scissors
* nail
* cotton string or shoelace
* soil
* plants
* water
* fertilizer
* science journal and pencil

1 With an adult's help, cut off the top of the soda bottle about one-third of the way down.

2 Also with an adult's help, use the nail to poke a hole through the center of the bottle cap.

3 Wet the cotton string or shoelace. Thread it through the hole in the cap. Part of it should be sticking out of the top and part out of the bottom. Screw the cap back on to the top of the bottle.

4 Fill the bottom part of the plastic bottle with water.

5 Turn the top part of the bottle upside down and place it in the bottom part. Making sure the shoelace stays upright (like a candlewick), fill the top part with soil, then put the plant of your choice in the soil.

6 Water your plant a little bit every day. Observe what happens to the water in the bottom container.

7 Add fertilizer to your plant. What happens to the water then?

8 Does algae grow in the water? How long does it take to grow?

TRY THIS! Instead of adding fertilizer to your plant, try adding something to the water—oil! Does this affect the plant's growth? How?

GROWING PLANTS

There are a lot of factors that affect how submerged plants grow, including the light, the clearness of the water, water temperature, and the available nutrients in the water. Sediment stability is important, too. If the sediment is disturbed too much by water patterns or wind, submerged plants can't thrive.

PROJECT!

PLANTS AND POLLUTION

Wetland plants are often the front line for absorbing pollutants from groundwater and other sources. Start a scientific method worksheet and find out how pollutants can affect them with this simple experiment.

SUPPLIES

* clear cups
* water
* dirt
* food coloring
* cut white flowers (such as Gerber daisies or mums)
* science journal and pencil

1 Fill two clear cups with water. In one cup, mix in some dirt and food coloring. Leave the other cup with only water. Place a cut flower in each cup.

2 Observe both flowers over the course of the next few days. Record your observations in your science journal.

- What do you notice?

- How long does it take for the flower in dirty water to change colors?

- How long does it take for it to wilt?

- How does it compare to the flower in clean water?

THINK ABOUT IT! What does this experiment tell you about the effect of water quality on wetland plants? How will the organisms that eat these plants be affected by the water quality?

PROJECT!

DECOMPOSITION

SUPPLIES

* soil
* dead leaves and small twigs
* worms or small beetles (optional)
* water
* microscope

Decomposition is an important part of the nutrient cycle that takes place in marshes and swamps. Start a scientific method worksheet and try your own decomposition project with the same bottle setup you used previously.

1 Follow steps 1–4 of the activity on page 38, "Get Growing." Turn the top part of the bottle upside down and place it in the bottom part. Making sure the shoelace stays upright (like a candlewick), fill this portion of the bottle with dead leaves and small twigs. You can also add some worms or beetles!

2 Place your bottle outside where it will receive plenty of air and sunlight. Observe what happens as the days pass. You might notice very small changes at first. Barely visible fungi or bacteria—possibly looking like white or black fuzz—could begin to form on the materials. Is the fuzz slimy? Does it attract insects?

3 Use a microscope to inspect the water in the bottom chamber. Do you see any microscopic animals? What shapes are they? Are these producers, consumers, or decomposers?

THINK ABOUT IT! What you're seeing is a miniature version of what happens in wetlands. The decomposition of plant life in marshes and swamps helps to feed living organisms, from **microbes** to shellfish, which in turn feed other organisms.

WORDS TO KNOW

microbe: a living thing too small to be seen without a microscope. Also called a microorganism.

41

PROJECT!

WHAT'S IN THE WATER?

How do pollutants from human activity affect water quality? Start a scientific method worksheet and do your own home experiment to find out, using materials from the hardware, home improvement, or grocery store.

SUPPLIES

* 6 mason jars (or any glass jar with a lid)
* water
* teaspoon
* laundry detergent
* plant fertilizer
* vinegar
* labels
* science journal and pencil

1 For your experiment, find a window ledge or table that receives sunlight most of the day.

2 Fill each jar with water. In each jar, place the following substances:

- **Jar 1:** 1 teaspoon of laundry detergent

- **Jar 2:** 1 teaspoon of plant fertilizer

- **Jar 3:** 5 teaspoons of plant fertilizer

- **Jar 4:** 1 teaspoon of vinegar

- **Jar 5:** 5 teaspoons of vinegar

- **Jar 6:** Just water

3 Label each jar so that you remember what's in it.

4 Keep the jars in the same place for one to two weeks, observing them daily.

FOCUS ON CANDABA

You can find Candaba Swamp in the Philippines, and there you can spot many migratory birds! The Shrenck's bittern, great bittern, Eurasian spoonbill, purple swamphen, Chinese pond heron, and black-crowned heron are a few of the bird species that winter there in the freshwater ponds and marshes. However, in recent years, the farmland around the swamp has been draining its waters earlier so rice can be grown instead of watermelons, and this is affecting the birds that rely on the area for food and shelter. What do you think? Should farmers try to change their practices? Should they risk their businesses to save the wetlands and the animals there?

5 Write down your observations in your science journal. Ask yourself some of the following questions.

- When does the algae start to grow? In which jar does most algae grow? How do the different materials affect its growth?

- How did the amount of the substance change the outcome? Was there a difference between a small amount of fertilizer or vinegar and a larger amount? What about the laundry detergent?

- How is the environment in your jars different from the environment in marshes and swamps?

THINK ABOUT IT! What do you think would happen if you added plants to your jars? What role could the plants play in the water?

PROJECT!

SALTY SOLUTIONS

Salt marshes are places where the salt water from the sea comes inland and feeds a thriving ecosystem. In these areas, the water is usually brackish, a mix of salt water and fresh water. As sea levels rise due to climate change, the marshes are getting saltier. Start a scientific method worksheet and see what effect increased salinity has on marsh plants.

1 Add a thin layer of gravel for drainage in each container, then fill them with soil and plant your seeds according to the instructions on the seed packet. Plant more than one seed per container in case some of the seeds don't take. Label the containers "Water," "Salt," or "Salt x 2."

2 Place your containers in a warm place where the seeds will get as many hours of sunlight as possible per day. Water the seeds daily, watering one container with water, one with water that has 1 teaspoon of salt mixed in, and one with water that has 2 teaspoons of salt.

3 During the course of your experiment, note the growth in each seed container. Record your observations in your science journal. How does the salt affect the growth of the seed? How long does it take each plant to grow as large as it can? What do you think this means for plants in a salt marsh?

THINK ABOUT IT: How would plant growth in the salt marsh affect other parts of the food web? How would it affect the animals that live in the marsh? Do you think different animals would start to live in the marsh if the water had more salt content?

CHAPTER 3

MARSH AND SWAMP CREATURES

We've learned that wetlands have been called "nature's kidneys," but did you know wetlands have also been called "nature's pantry" and "nature's nursery"? Wetlands provide lots of food and make wonderful homes for animals of all kinds.

Because wetlands have so many benefits for animals, they attract a wide variety of species. With so many different types of animals living in the same places, it's not surprising that animals themselves can have different roles.

Some are predators. Some are prey. Some can be both at different times!

WORDS TO KNOW

predator: an animal that hunts another animal for food.

WHAT'S ON THE MENU?

The plants that grow in marshes and swamps—and later decompose—provide food for all kinds of different animals, from crabs to frogs. Larger animals in the wetlands eat smaller animals. Because wetlands release water even during drought periods, marshes and swamps can be a source of food when it's hard to find food in other places.

?

INVESTIGATE!

Why is it important to have both predators and prey living in an ecosystem?

ALLIGATOR ATTACK! NOT.

Alligators have a bad reputation. But alligator attacks on humans are rare. Alligators will not attack humans unless provoked or they sense a threat to their environment or their offspring. Like many other creatures, they simply want to be left in peace to raise their young and eat.

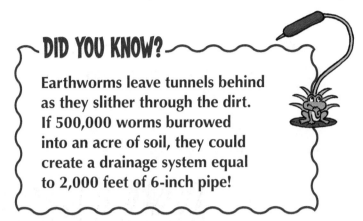

DID YOU KNOW?

Earthworms leave tunnels behind as they slither through the dirt. If 500,000 worms burrowed into an acre of soil, they could create a drainage system equal to 2,000 feet of 6-inch pipe!

detritus-eater: also known as a detritivore, an organism that eats dead plant material.

metamorphosis: the process some animals go through in their life cycle. They change size, shape, and color.

WORDS TO KNOW

Marsh and swamp animals include both predators and detritus-eaters. Predators eat other creatures. One of the best-known swamp predators is the alligator. These creatures can grow up to 15 feet long and weigh up to 700 pounds. They eat snakes, fish, turtles, small animals, and even baby alligators!

Detritus-eaters, also known as detritivores, eat decomposed plant and waste material or the bacteria that grows in water. One detritivore you might know about is the earthworm. These slithery creatures live in the soil and feed on both live and dead organic matter. As earthworms feed and deposit their waste, they add even more nutrients to the soil. Snails are another example of a detritivore!

ANIMAL LIFE CYCLES

Marshes and swamps are important for animals during different stages in their life cycles. Because they are safe places, insects use the stalks and leaves of plants during metamorphosis.

MARSHES AND SWAMPS!

molting: the process in which a bird's old feathers are pushed out by new feathers growing in.

vulnerable: exposed to harm.

roost: a place where birds settle to rest.

WORDS ⊙ KNOW

Waterfowl often hide among the reeds and grasses while they are molting. When birds molt, they are more vulnerable to predators than usual since they can't fly. Wetlands offer places to hide from predators until the birds' feathers grow back and they can fly again.

Marshes and swamps provide a resting and feeding stop for migrating birds. Some types of birds will roost in these places and raise their young until they are ready to continue their migratory journey.

Many reptiles and birds lay their eggs in the protected areas of marshes and swamps. The tall grasses provide protection from predators for small creatures.

DID YOU KNOW?

The number of birds migrating over the Gulf of Mexico that rely on coastal wetlands has decreased by one-half since the mid-1960s.

PS Check out this interactive map of migrating birds!

KEYWORD PROMPTS

National Geographic migrating birds path

YOU ARE WHAT YOU EAT

Pink wetlands birds such as the flamingo and the roseate spoonbill get their beautiful color from the food they eat. A natural substance enters their systems and turns them pink through the brine shrimp and blue-green algae that make up most of their diet. Baby flamingos are actually born with gray feathers!

Different kinds of fish and amphibians also spawn in marshes and swamps. Many types of fish, including largemouth bass, northern pike, and chain pickerel, live in deeper, more open water and come to marshes to spawn. There's plenty of food for babies, and the thick emergent plants provide protection.

Frogs also lay their eggs in wetlands. You might find a bunch of frog eggs in a jelly-like mass! This jelly-like substance keeps the eggs moist and protected.

CAN YOU SPOT THE FROG EGGS?

WHAT DID YOU FIND?

Here are some of the organisms you'll find in wetlands! Visit a wetland and see how many of these you spot signs of.

INSECTS: Insects might be on the surface of the water, flying over the water, or sitting on the stalks, stems, or leaves of plants near the water. You may see them on dry ground, on tree trunks, or on logs.

FROGS, TOADS, NEWTS, AND SALAMANDERS: Look in the plants near the water, on logs in or near the water, or on rocks near the water. Salamanders can often be found under rocks in the water.

TURTLES: Turtles might be swimming under the surface of the water swimming, sitting on logs or rocks in the water, or sitting on the banks.

SNAILS: They may be on rocks, plants, or logs.

DID YOU KNOW?

Some animals, such as fish and turtles, hibernate in the bottom of ponds or in standing water during the winter.

PS Creatures of the ocean and wetlands often have a lot in common and can encounter each other in coastal wetlands or during migration. **Learn more about your favorite species here!**

KEYWORD PROMPTS

NOAA fisheries

MINNOWS: These baby fish can be seen swimming close to the banks in the water.

TADPOLES: These baby frogs can be seen in the water in the springtime.

WHAT DO YOU GET WHEN YOU CROSS A TURTLE WITH A PORCUPINE?

A slow poke!

PLANTS: Look for different kinds of plants both in and near the water. Do you see any shrubs or trees? That can help you decide if an area is a marsh or swamp (see page 4).

ANIMAL TRACKS: Do you see any tracks in the mud near the water? That may give you a clue about animals that have visited the area but like to stay out of sight of humans!

FISH: While fish are secretive, you may be able to see a few moving around not far below the surface of the water.

BIRDS: You might see birds overhead or in the reeds or grasses.

What about humans? While few of us live in marshes and swamps, wetlands are incredibly important for humans, and many human activities are having harmful effects on marshes and swamps. We'll learn more about this in the next chapter.

? CONSIDER AND DISCUSS

It's time to consider and discuss: Why is it important to have both predators and prey living in an ecosystem?

PROJECT!

WHO LIVES HERE?

Wetland animals can be secretive. But if you know where to look and look closely, you can find traces of them! For this project, you'll need to go to a wetland to do some fieldwork.

SUPPLIES

* science journal and pencil
* tracking guide from the library or the internet
* collecting bag or pouch

Caution: Always bring an adult with you when you visit a wetland.

1 Although they are secretive, wetland animals will leave signs of themselves behind. Start by looking down. Do you see tracks in the wet ground? Check the tracks against a track guide. Think about when the tracks were made. What time of day do you think the animal visited this area?

2 Look in the plants, trees, and underbrush for telltale signs of local animals. Are there nests in the trees, shrubs, or grasses? Does it look like a nest has been abandoned? If so, are there pieces of broken eggshells in the nest? That could mean a baby was born in the nest and has now grown up and moved away! The nest could also be home to a different type of animal, such as a mink or an alligator, depending on the region you are in.

3 Look at the stems of plants, from top to bottom. Are there shells near or on the plant? If so, the animal that lives in the shell may be feeding!

4 Look for feathers or discarded shells. Check the rules of the wetland you are visiting to see if it's okay to collect them. Never take a shell that has a living animal inside it!

PROJECT!

A BEAVER MADE THIS DAM!

5 If the marsh or swamp you visit has standing water, look for eggs from fish or frogs. You'll find these only in the spring time. Be careful not to disturb the eggs! You might also see insect eggs in the water. Look for piles of sticks or branches. This could be a sign that beavers have been building dams.

6 Are there fallen trees in the wetland you visit? Look for hollows in the trees or under the roots. These places could be home to animals such as alligators or minks, depending on where you are visiting. Look for telltale signs of beavers in the tree's trunk. A beaver's teeth will leave chewing marks!

7 Record all your findings in your science journal and name as many of the animals as you can!

TRY THIS! If you can, visit a different wetland and compare what you see there to what you found in the first one. Are there signs of different animals? Different vegetation?

PROJECT!

FOCUS ON THE FOOD WEB

SUPPLIES

* index cards
* several pieces of string
* colored markers

In marshes and swamps, almost everything is on the menu! This activity focuses on predators and detritus eaters. These animals are part of the food web. See if you can connect the animals to their sources of food!

1 Using your library or the internet, research the organisms on this list. What do they eat? What eats them?

- raccoon
- blue crab
- fish
- egret
- person
- shrimp
- snail

- oyster
- fiddler crab
- mallard duck
- osprey
- kingfisher
- mink
- muskrat

- alligator
- marsh grass
- shallow pond vegetation
- cattail
- mushrooms
- bacteria

2 Write each organism's name on an index card and write facts about it on the other side of the card. Lay the cards out on a table.

3 Using pieces of string, make lines between an animal and its food source. More than one animal can be connected to a single source. Use different colored markers to show what an animal eats and who eats it!

THINK ABOUT IT! What does your food web tell you about the relationships between animals in wetlands?

PROJECT!

A TANGLED WEB

As you've learned, the food web is one of the most important factors in a marsh or swamp. If one species changes or declines, it affects all the others. Every species is important! Do your own experiment to see how one species affects others.

SUPPLIES

* pictures of organisms from page 54 or from the internet
* poster board
* glue
* string
* strong tape
* scissors

1 Glue your animal pictures in no particular order in a large circle around the edges of the poster board. Make eyelets out of the tape so you have small holes that string can move through smoothly.

2 Starting with one organism, tape the end of a piece of string to the picture, then pull the string to the picture of an animal that it eats. Tape an eyelet on that picture and thread the string through. Don't cut it. Continue to unroll the string, threading it through an eyelet on the picture of the organism that that organism eats. Try to keep the string tight. You are building a web.

3 Once you have strings connecting the organisms, snip the yarn connecting one organism to another. Notice that the string will slacken throughout the web. What does this tell you about the food web and all the animals it involves?

THINK ABOUT IT: Look at each organism. Consider what might threaten each one, and in turn threaten the whole food web. How are the members of the food web reliant on each other?

SUPPLIES

✳ Poster board
✳ Markers

LIFE IN THE MARSH MATCHING GAME

Marshes and swamps are ever-changing places. Some animals are born in water but can live on land. Some stay in the water. Some animals migrate from wetlands to other places. Some stay in the wetland. Some animals hibernate. Some don't.

Research the behavior of each animal on the following page, then divide the animals into the correct categories. Some animals can be in more than one category!

Categories

- Land dwellers
- Water dwellers
- Land and water dwellers

- Nesters
- Migrators
- Hibernators

SNORE

When turtles hibernate, they don't actually sleep. Their whole system slows down and their body needs very little energy to stay alive and healthy. But they still need some energy to stay alive! They use energy that they have stored in their bodies. They take in oxygen from the pond water where they hibernate through their rear ends!

PROJECT!

Marsh and swamp animals

- Alligator
- Bat
- Beaver
- Blue crab
- Bobcat
- Caddis fly
- Canada goose
- Damselfly
- Dragonfly
- Deer
- Duck
- Fiddler crab
- Fox
- Frog
- Egret
- Hawk
- Heron
- Kingfisher
- Mallard
- Mink

- Newt
- Opossum
- Osprey
- Otter
- Oyster
- Owl
- Rabbit
- Raccoon
- Shrimp
- Slug
- Snake
- Snail
- Swallow
- Toad
- Turtle

DID YOU KNOW?

Marshes and swamps provide shelter for many types of animals. Aquatic animals, insects, and invertebrates are drawn to the watery areas. Birds nest in the grasses, shrubs, and trees.

PROJECT!

FLYWAY FEVER

SUPPLIES

* ✳ poster board
* ✳ markers
* ✳ dice
* ✳ game chips (use plastic model birds or create your own birds with paper or clay)

When migrating birds follow their annual migration paths, they choose routes or "flyways" that take them over water—rivers, marshes, swamps, and other wetlands. In these places, birds stop to eat, roost, and give birth to their babies. But along a bird's path, obstacles can keep it from getting to its destination. Create a board game to understand a bird's challenges.

1 On one end of your board, write "Winter Habitat." You can use markers to illustrate this area, indicating what it might look like—reeds, grasses, water, or something else. One the other end of the board, write "Summer Habitat." What will you illustrate here?

2 Between these two points, draw a snaking "flyway" that looks like a twisting, turning, block path—the kind you might see in common board games. Make the blocks big enough to write on. When you're done, your board should look something like this:

PROJECT!

3 Along the way, place obstacles and rewards for your birds. Here are some examples.

* Uh-oh! A new housing development! Your wetland was drained. Move back four spaces

* This wetland is polluted and the fish you eat have died! Move back two spaces.

* Oh, no, an oil spill! You can't land. Move back two spaces.

* A drought! Move back one space.

* An invasive species was introduced to your habitat. Move back three spaces

* Good news! Your wetland was restored! Move ahead four spaces.

* A new wetland was created! Move ahead three spaces.

* An invasive species was removed! Move ahead two spaces.

* New nesting boxes! Move ahead three spaces.

* People planted nesting covers! Move ahead two spaces.

4 Place your game pieces in the summer habitat area of the board. With another player, take turns rolling one of the dice and moving ahead. Whoever gets to the winter habitat first wins!

TRY THIS! After you finish the game, discuss all the obstacles that the birds needed to overcome to get to the "finish line." These are real problems that migrating birds face each year. Then discuss the positive factors. Many of them involved the help of people. Talk about what you might be able to do in your community to help migrating birds on their annual journeys.

PROJECT!

OBSERVING SPECIMENS

SUPPLIES

* science journal and pencil
* glass jar
* 2 clear rectangular plastic containers
* eyedropper
* ice cube trays
* magnifying glass
* plastic bags
* small net

Specimens **are examples of a type of organism used for scientific study. By looking at a single specimen, you can get an idea of what that type of organism is like in general. Look at underwater specimens at your local marsh or swamp. Be sure to follow the rules and return the organism to its place after you finish making your observations.**

Caution: Always bring an adult with you when you visit a wetland.

1 Start by noting the date, place, and time in your science journal. Note the current state of the water. How does it look? Is it clear or does it look muddy?

2 Use the glass jar to fill a plastic container with water. Allow the water to settle. What do you see? You will probably spot many things moving around, such as stoneflies, mayfly nymphs, crane flies, and mosquito larvae.

3 Use the eyedropper to pull up a few drops of water containing these organisms. Transfer the organisms to a section of the ice cube tray, along with some of the water. Use a magnifying glass to get a better look.

4 What do you observe? What does it look like? How does it move? How big is it? Use your notebook to jot down your observations about each organism. Draw pictures of them in your journal, too.

WORDS TO KNOW

specimen: a sample used for study.

PROJECT!

FOCUS ON THE PANTANAL

The Pantanal is a tropical wetland that lies across the countries of Brazil, Paraguay, and Bolivia. It's one of the world's largest wetlands! During the rainy season, about 80 percent of the wetland is under water, which means there's lots of aquatic life making use of this environment, including the apple snail. This interesting creature has both lungs and gills, which means it can live both above water and below water.

5 Be sure to return your specimens to the water after you finish observing them! You can repeat your observations at a different time of year to see if the type and number of organisms in the water are different.

THINK ABOUT IT! Consider the type of water in which you found your specimens. Was it moving or still? Was it a vernal pool? What does your specimen need to live in this water? Do you think your specimen would be able to live in a different type of water?

So, you found several tiny creatures in the water. What are they? **I Spot Nature has a great guide to help you find out!**

KEYWORD PROMPTS

ispotnature

CHAPTER 4

WARNING SIGNS AND WETLAND THREATS

· ·

You now know how important marshes and swamps are in providing animal habitats, preventing flooding and erosion, storing groundwater, and filtering pollutants from water. All of these functions make wetlands one of the most important types of ecosystems.

· ·

But marshes and swamps face many threats, including draining and in-fill from development, pollution, and invasive species of plants and animals.

? INVESTIGATE!

How might climate change affect the area you live in?

In addition to threats on a local level, marshes and swamps are greatly affected by climate change. Environmental problems such as rising sea levels are often felt first in coastal marshes. And just like in a food web, when part of these delicate systems is affected, the entire system is changed.

CLIMATE CHANGE

WORDS ⊙ KNOW

draining: removing water from wetlands in order to use the land for development or other human activity.

in-fill: when marshes or swamps are filled in with new soil to remove their moisture.

sea level: the level of the surface of the sea.

Do you ever hear people complain that a summer was too hot or a winter too cold? The temperatures they are talking about aren't an indication of climate change, though they might be related.

Climate change is the change in the average worldwide temperature across long periods of time. Scientists have discovered that the average temperature of the earth is rising and that it has been rising more quickly in recent years than in the past.

DID YOU KNOW?

Even a small rise in sea level can cause flooding in coastal areas. Around the world, one in 10 people lives in a coastal area that is less than 30 feet above sea level.

(PS) You can track the earth's temperature on this interactive map. **What do you think the map will look like in the next decade?**

KEYWORD PROMPTS

NASA world of change 🔍

greenhouse gas: a gas in the atmosphere that traps heat. We need some greenhouse gases, but too many trap too much heat and cause climate change.

fossil fuels: energy sources such as coal, oil, and natural gas that come from plants and animals that lived millions of year ago.

WORDS TO KNOW

WHAT GAME DO FISH LIKE TO PLAY AT PARTIES?

Salmon Says

One of the main causes of climate change has been the increase in greenhouse gases in the earth's atmosphere. Greenhouse gases are caused in part by the burning of fossil fuels.

People burn fossil fuels for heat and energy. Greenhouse gases, including carbon dioxide and methane, trap heat in the earth's atmosphere. The ocean absorbs much of the extra heat caused by greenhouse gases. In fact, the surface layer of the ocean stores as much heat as the earth's entire atmosphere!

As a result of this extra heat, ocean temperatures around the world are rising. This can create many problems.

For example, higher ocean temperatures mean polar ice sheets melt. All the water in the polar ice sheet needs somewhere to go—the ocean! This makes sea levels rise. A higher sea level affects coastlines, coastal communities, and coastal wetlands.

ON THE SHORE

polar ice sheet: one of several sheets of ice found in the Arctic and Antarctica.

encroach: advance into or enter a territory.

aquifer: an underground layer of rock that has space in it that holds water. In many places, this is where drinking water comes from.

WORDS ⊙ KNOW

One way that rising sea levels affect coastal wetlands is through shoreline erosion. As dunes and beaches erode, salty water encroaches into coastal wetlands. This makes the water saltier. There could be increased salinity in wetlands, rivers, and aquifers.

COASTAL FLOODING

About 40 percent of the world's population lives within 62 miles of the ocean. Because climate change is bringing higher tides and higher storm surges, these people and their property are at risk. Barrier islands, beaches, sand dunes, salt marshes, and mangrove stands get pushed further inland as sea levels rise. Sometimes, whole communities are forced to move.

(PS) You can see the coastal city of Boston, Massachusetts, getting flooded at this website.

KEYWORD PROMPTS

NBC Boston flood 🔍

Saltier water can affect both plants and animals living in wetlands. Not all the plants and animals living in these areas can survive increased salinity. As you've learned, a change to one part of the food web or habitat can hurt organisms throughout the ecosystem.

Climate change can also lead to more coastal flooding. Although wetlands have always functioned as a barrier against flooding, they have limits! Too much water can cause wetlands to overflow and flood the surrounding area.

Climate change has serious and long-term effects on wetlands. In the next chapter, you'll learn how you can help to protect them yourself!

?

CONSIDER AND DISCUSS

It's time to consider and discuss: How might climate change affect the area you live in?

(PS) Scientists use maps when studying wetlands. **You can find maps that illustrate different types of landforms and ecosystems on this website.** They also have maps that illustrate reports on the health of the environment.

KEYWORD PROMPTS

USGS maps 🔍

PROJECT!

CAN THIS WETLAND BE SAVED?

Pollutants such as pesticides and oil damage wetlands every day. But can that damage be undone? Start a scientific method worksheet and try this project to discover how pollutants can have long-term effects on water.

Caution: Have an adult help you choose which garbage to use—stay away from anything that is sharp or contains chemicals.

1 Fill your large plastic container with water. Wearing plastic gloves, add items from your garbage into the water. This could include food waste, packaging, paper towels—whatever is in your garbage at the moment. Add vegetable oil to the water.

2 Now, remove the garbage from the container, using the tongs and strainer to pick them up and put them on the lid of the container.

3 After you remove everything you can from the water, observe it. What stayed in the water despite your effort to remove it? What does that tell you about the effects of pollution?

THINK ABOUT IT! Consider the filtering properties of wetlands. If they are damaged or the plants there are choked out by invasive species, what will happen to the pollution in the water?

WORDS TO KNOW

pesticide: a chemical used to kill pests such as insects.

67

PROJECT!

OIL SPILL!

SUPPLIES

* ✳ science journal and pencil
* ✳ 3 small pans
* ✳ water
* ✳ liquid soap
* ✳ vegetable oil
* ✳ 3 feathers
* ✳ toothbrush or kitchen sponge

According to the U.S. National Oceanic and Administration Agency, more than 100 major oil spills take place each year. Daily, however, smaller amounts of oil enter waterways **through groundwater and industrial and agricultural runoff. Oil damages plants and animals in marshes and swamps, particularly birds. A bird's feathers are made from tiny strands of hair and "hooks." This design helps keep a bird warm and dry. When feathers get oily, they can't stay fluffed up and can't keep in warmth. Start a scientific method worksheet and try this project to find out how oil spills can harm birds' feathers.**

1 In your science journal, make three columns. At the top of each column, write one of these labels: "Absorbed," "Repelled," and "Changes." On the side of each column, create three rows and write "Water," "Liquid Soap," and "Oil."

2 Fill one pan with water, one pan with dish soap, and one with vegetable oil. Dip the first feather in the water. Observe. Does the feather absorb or repel the water? Record your observations in the correct column.

3 Dip the second feather in dish soap. What do you notice about the feather? Write your thoughts on your chart. Finally, dip the third feather in the vegetable oil. What happens to this feather?

WORDS TO KNOW

waterway: a channel or body of water.

4 Now, sprinkle water on the oil-soaked feather. Does the feather absorb or repel the water? Record your observations.

5 Dip the toothbrush or kitchen sponge in water and dish soap. Try to remove the oil with the soapy water and the toothbrush. What happens? Can you get the oil out?

THINK ABOUT IT: What does this experiment tell you about how oil affects feathers? Why is it important to keep oil out of our lakes, streams, and oceans?

SEA LEVEL RISE

SUPPLIES

* measuring cup
* modeling clay
* 2 clear plastic food containers
* water
* marker
* ice cubes

Wetlands all over the world are affected by the oceans. And oceans are affected by the polar ice caps. At the North Pole, the cap is floating ice. At the South Pole, ice lies in a sheet over the continent of Antarctica. When floating ice melts, the liquid water replaces the space taken up by the solid ice. When ice in an ice sheet melts and flows into the ocean, the sea level rises.

Climate change has caused long-term melt at both poles. Start a scientific method worksheet and try this experiment to see how melting polar ice caps can affect the planet.

1 Measure one cup of the modeling clay and put it in the center of one of the plastic containers. Shape the modeling clay into a mound. Flatten the top of the mound. This represents the South Pole. Label the side of the container "South Pole."

2 Label the side of the second container "North Pole" and fill it about two-thirds full with water. Add two ice cubes to the water and quickly mark the level of the water with a marker on the side of the container. This container represents the North Pole and its floating ice.

3 Add water around the mound of the South Pole until the water comes about two-thirds of the way up its side. Mark the side of the container with a marker to show the current water level.

WORDS TO KNOW

polar ice cap: a dome-shaped sheet of ice found at both the North and South Poles.

4 Put two ice cubes on the flat top of the South Pole, pressing them into the clay to keep them in place.

5 Let your two poles sit. Observe the melting ice. After all the ice has melted, check the water level in the containers. What happened? Have the water levels risen? Why or why not?

THINK ABOUT IT! What do your results demonstrate? What is the difference between the floating ice of the North Pole and sheet of ice at the South Pole?

PROJECT!

SALTY WATERS

SUPPLIES

* 2 glass jars
* measuring spoons
* water
* salt
* spoon
* food thermometer
* food coloring
* science journal and pencil

As more ocean waters mix with coastal wetland waters, salt marshes will contain more and more salt. This can be very harmful to the plants and animals that live there, which may not be able to adapt to the higher levels of salt. Start a scientific method worksheet and let's see how.

1 In one glass jar, mix 8 ounces of cold water with 4 teaspoons of salt. Measure the temperature of the water and write it in your science journal. This water represents cold water found at the North and South Poles.

2 In the second jar, mix 4 teaspoons of salt with room temperature water. Measure the temperature of the water and record it in your science journal. This represents warmer water flowing into polar water.

FOCUS ON THE BANGWEULU SWAMPS

The Bangweulu Swamps in Zambia is considered to be one of the world's most important wetlands. This is because it's home to many species of birds and animals, including the fruit bat, shoebill, wattled crane, lechwe, and sable antelope. Plus, about 50,000 to 90,000 people depend on this wetland for farming and fishing. Several organizations are working on conservation efforts to ensure a relationship between humans and the land that is helpful and lasting for everyone, not just today's farmers and fishermen. The name Bangweulu means "where the water sky meets the sky."

WORDS TO KNOW

adapt: changes a plant or animal makes to survive in new or different conditions.

PROJECT!

3 Add several drops of food coloring to the room temperature water and stir.

4 Pour the room temperature water into a spoon placed over the jar of cold water. Let that water slowly spill into the cold water. What happens to the cold water? Where does it go?

5 Pour out your warm water. Add even warmer water to the jar, as well as more salt. Pour that water into the cold water jar in the same way as before and observe what happens.

THINK ABOUT IT: How does increasingly warmer, saltier water affect the cold water? How might it affect creatures that live there? How will that affect what they eat and the greater food web?

PROJECT!

THERMAL EXPANSION

As the earth's temperature increases, sea levels rise. This is because of thermal expansion, the ways matter changes in response to a change in temperature. What effect will that have on coastal areas, including the marshes and swamps around them? Start a scientific method worksheet and try this experiment.

1 Fill the first jar with very cold water. Pour a little food coloring into the water to help you see the results of your experiment.

2 Use the nail to make two holes in the lid. The holes need to be big enough for the thermometer and glass tube. Place the thermometer and glass tube into the jar through the holes. The water will rise up into the glass tube to a certain point.

3 Record the temperature of the water. On the side of the glass tube, mark the water line. Place the jar near the lamp. The light should be facing the water, not the top of the jar.

4 In about 10 minutes, check the temperature of the water and the position of the water in the tube. What do you notice about the temperature? What do you notice about the water inside the tube?

SUPPLIES

* glass jars with lids
* water
* food coloring
* nail
* a thin glass tube, open on each end
* long thermometer
* lamp
* marker
* science journal and pencil

THINK ABOUT IT:
What do you think your findings mean for sea level rise? What do they mean for coastal communities? For marshes and swamps located near the ocean?

WORDS TO KNOW

thermal expansion: the ways matter changes in response to a change in temperature.

matter: what an object is made of. Anything that has weight and takes up space.

74

CHAPTER 5

PROTECTING MARSHES AND SWAMPS

Kids can make a real difference to the environment. For example, in 1995, children from a Minnesota elementary school conducted some fieldwork and discovered frogs in their local wetland that were deformed. Some had legs in the wrong places and others had too many legs or eyes.

When they reported their findings to the Minnesota Pollution Control Agency, scientists found that the same kinds of deformities existed in frogs in nearby areas. During the next few years, scientists found more than 13,000 frogs with similar problems! And it all started with kids.

? INVESTIGATE!

What can you do to help keep wetlands healthy in your town?

MARSHES AND SWAMPS!

Now that you know how important wetlands are, you are in a great position to help protect them.

CHANGE YOUR CONSUMER HABITS

You can help the environment in lots of ways every day. One way is to try to use less water in your house. This will help decrease the stress on the water resources in your area, which will help wetlands. Saving water also helps reduce the amount of water going into sewage treatment plants.

Use paper and recycled products made from unbleached paper. Bleached paper contains more chemicals that can contaminate water. When we keep bleach out of the waste stream, we help to reduce pollution in wetlands.

Ask your parents to follow organic methods for yard and garden care. Chemicals and pesticides get washed into nearby streams or ponds and into the groundwater when it rains. These connect to our wetlands and harm plants and animals.

Try to encourage helpful bugs, such as ladybugs, hoverflies, and ground beetles, to come live in your garden. They will take care of the harmful bugs on their own! In your yard, use only native plants. Invasive species can quickly become a problem for local plants.

MAKE A DIFFERENCE IN YOUR COMMUNITY

Not only can you help the environment in your own backyard, you can help your community, too! Check with a local environmental organization to find out when a wetland cleanup is happening. If one isn't scheduled, offer to organize one and involve your friends or classmates.

BECOME A CITIZEN SCIENTIST

Citizen science helps to protect the environment! Professional scientists depend on people such as you to monitor wetlands and collect data about what's happening in marshes, swamps, and waterways. Citizen scientists help scientists to discover things that individual scientists could never achieve on their own.

To learn more about freshwater wetlands, you can download several free maps and apps from this website.

KEYWORD PROMPTS

wikiwatershed 🔍

Help plant trees with a local environmental group. Trees, shrubs, and groundcovers reduce runoff that can be full of chemicals and harm the water.

Volunteer with a local park or protected area. Projects such as building nesting platforms for migratory birds can have a real impact, and park staff is always looking for help with ways to improve bird habitats!

EDUCATE OTHERS!

One great way to help the environment is to raise public awareness. In Ohio, for example, a group of kids wanted to protect spotted salamanders, whose habitat is at risk. They wrote to a state senator and asked him to make the salamander the official state amphibian.

WHY WOULDN'T THE SHRIMP SHARE HIS TREASURE?

Because he was a little shellfish!

The kids went to the statehouse and testified about the importance of the salamander. They shared facts they had learned about the salamander, including many things the lawmakers didn't know. They were able to raise awareness about this important creature at a high level in government!

Plan a wetland program or invite a wetland expert to speak at your school. World Wetlands Day on February 2 is a great time to plan activities. May is also American Wetlands Month! State, local, and national parks sponsor activities during this time, including guided walks in wetlands, cleanups, and introductions to water monitoring.

Finally, get out and enjoy wetlands near you! Go for a walk, go bird watching, go canoeing or kayaking, or do some scientific research. When you experience how amazing wetlands are, you can be a great spokesperson for protecting them!

? CONSIDER AND DISCUSS

It's time to consider and discuss: What can you do to help keep wetlands healthy in your town?

PS Are you curious about what's in the water you drink? **Check out the US Geological Survey's Water Science School!**

KEYWORD PROMPTS

Water Science School 🔍

PROJECT!

BUILD A BACKYARD WETLAND

One of the best ways to learn about how to protect and nurture a marsh or swamp is to create your own. No matter where you live, you can make your own "pocket wetland" in your garden or backyard, if you've got a little land. Don't be discouraged if this doesn't work at first—all gardeners experience challenges!

> **Caution:** You must have permission from an adult to create this wetland.

1 Look around your yard or garden. Is there a spot that usually stays somewhat wet? This could be a place where there is a natural area. This would be an ideal spot for your pocket wetland. When picking a place, follow these guidelines.

- It should be away from the foundation of your house.

- If you will need to add water to this spot, it must be reachable by garden hose.

- Your wetland should not affect your neighbors.

2 Decide what size and shape you'd like your wetland to be. Start small. An irregular shape will appear the most natural. Even if you have a long, narrow area, it can still be a wetland.

3 If your spot is not currently in a low area, you will need to dig it out. Dig about 1½ to 2 feet deep with sloping sides.

4 If the area has good drainage, line the bottom of the hole with a plastic liner to keep the area moist. Hold the liner in place with heavy stones. If you live in an area that receives a lot of rainfall, puncture the liner in several places with pencil-sized holes to allow for some drainage and to prevent the area from staying too wet. If the area stays moist anyway, line the bottom with gravel or sand.

5 Fill your hole with a mix of peat and humus. These kinds of soil will help retain moisture in your wetland.

6 Think about what plants you want to plant in your wetland and consult an expert at your local plant nursery to find out what the best native wetland plants are for your area. Unless your wetland is going to be continually wet, you probably won't be able to use bog plants. You'll want your plants to be tolerant of wet soil and have shallow root systems. Go for a mix of plants.

Flowering plants for sunny, moist, or boggy conditions

- Cattails
- Joe-Pye weed
- Great blue lobelia
- Ironweed
- Goldenrods
- Marsh marigold
- Swamp milkweed
- Gentian

PROJECT CONTINUED ON NEXT PAGE . . .

PROJECT!

Native plants for shady, moist, or boggy conditions

- Bee balm
- Arrowhead
- False hellebore
- Skunk cabbage

- Royal fern
- Netted chain fern
- Jack-in-the-Pulpit
- Turtlehead

True bog plants

- Sundews
- Butterworts

- Pitcher plants

7 Once your wetland is planted, make sure to keep it moist. Unless you live in a very rainy area, you will need to water it. Check the ground for moisture every few days. You may need to choose some different types of plants if the ones you originally plant don't take. Don't give up!

8 Observe your wetland. What kind of insects or birds are attracted to it? Have you noticed any other wildlife in the area? Use your science journal to keep track of your wetland in different seasons.

TRY THIS! If you can, consider expanding your wetland to add a water feature, such as a pond. You'll attract more wildlife and will be able to make more observations.

A

absorb: to soak up.

adapt: changes a plant or animal makes to survive in new or different conditions.

algae: a plant-like organism that turns light into energy. Algae does not have leaves or roots.

amphibian: an animal with moist skin that is born in water but lives on land. An amphibian changes its body temperature by moving to warmer or cooler places. Frogs, toads, newts, efts, and salamanders are amphibians.

aquatic: living or growing in water.

aquifer: an underground layer of rock that has space in it that holds water. In many places, this is where drinking water comes from.

atmosphere: the mixture of gases surrounding the earth.

B

bacteria: tiny organisms found in animals, plants, soil, and water. Bacteria decompose dead plants and animals to make nutrients available as food for other organisms.

biodiverse: full of many different types of life.

bog: a wetland where plant material decomposes very slowly and builds up over time as peat.

brackish: water that contains a mix of salt water and fresh water.

C

carbon dioxide: a natural gas that's called a greenhouse gas. In excess, it contributes to the warming of the atmosphere.

carnivorous plant: a plant that traps and eats animals.

citizen science: the involvement of everyday people in scientific activities or projects.

climate: the average weather patterns in an area during a long period of time.

climate change: changes to the average weather patterns in an area during a long period of time.

conserve: to save or protect something, or to use it carefully so it isn't used up.

consumer: an organism that takes in food for energy. Organisms can be both producers and consumers.

contaminate: to pollute or make dirty.

D

debris: pieces of dead plants or branches.

decomposer: an organism that eats and breaks down dead plants and animals, providing nutrients to other living organisms.

decompose: to rot or decay.

detritus-eater: also known as a detritivore, an organism that eats dead plant material.

diverse: lots of different species.

draining: removing water from wetlands in order to use the land for development or other human activity.

drought: a long period of little or no rain.

dune: a mound or ridge of sand that has been blown by the wind.

E

ecosystem: a community of living and nonliving things and their environment. Living things are plants, animals, and insects. Nonliving things are soil, rocks, and water.

GLOSSARY

emergent plant: a plant that has roots sometimes or always underwater, with a body that extends out of the water.

encroach: advance into or enter a territory.

environment: a natural area with animals, plants, rocks, soil, and water.

erosion: the wearing away of a surface by wind, water, or other process.

evergreen: a plant that keeps its leaves or needles throughout the year.

excess: more than the normal amount.

F

fen: a wetland similar to a bog, except that it is fed by water from underground.

filterer: an animal that uses a filtering motion to feed. These animals include tiny animals such as krill and bigger animals such as whales.

floating-leaf plant: a plant that lives on the surface of the water.

flooding: when water covers an area that is usually dry.

food web: the interconnected system of feeding relationships in an ecosystem.

fossil fuels: energy sources such as coal, oil, and natural gas that come from plants and animals that lived millions of year ago.

fungus: a plant-like living thing without leaves or flowers. It grows on plants and things that are rotting, such as old logs. Examples are mold, mildew, and mushrooms. Plural is fungi.

G

greenhouse gas: a gas in the atmosphere that traps heat. We need some greenhouse gases, but too many trap too much heat and cause climate change.

groundwater: water that is held underground in the soil or in cracks and crevices in rocks.

H

habitat: the natural area where a plant or an animal lives.

hammock: an area of dry land rising out of a swamp.

hibernate: to go into a deep sleep for many months with a low body temperature and heart rate.

hydric: saturated with water for much of the year.

I

indicator species: a species that can be studied to understand the overall health of an ecosystem.

in-fill: when marshes or swamps are filled in with new soil to remove their moisture.

invasive species: a species that is not native to an ecosystem and that is harmful to the ecosystem in some way.

invertebrate: an animal without a backbone.

L

lichen: yellow, green, and gray plants that grow in patches on rocks, trees, and the ground.

life cycle: the growth and changes a living organism goes through from birth to death.

M

mammal: a type of animal, such as a human, dog, or cat. Mammals are born live, feed milk to their young, and usually have hair or fur covering most of their skin.

mangrove: a tree or shrub that grows in tropical coastal swamps.

marsh: an area of wet, low land with plants that like growing in water but that die back to the ground each winter.

84

matter: what an object is made of. Anything that has weight and takes up space.

metamorphosis: the process some animals go through in their life cycle. They change size, shape, and color.

microbe: a living thing too small to be seen without a microscope. Also called a microorganism.

migrate: to move from one environment to another when seasons change.

molting: the process in which a bird's old feathers are pushed out by new feathers growing in.

monitor: to watch, keep track of, or check.

moss: a small, seedless plant that grows in soft feathery patches in moist places, such as the ground of a thick forest.

muck: muddy, wet soil.

N

nutrient or nutrition cycle: the path a nutrient takes through one organism or element of the environment to the next.

nutrients: substances in food and soil that living things need to live and grow.

O

organic: something that is or was living, such as animals, wood, grass, and insects. Also refers to food grown naturally, without chemicals.

organism: any living thing.

P

peat: a substance formed from decomposing vegetation or other dead matter.

pesticide: a chemical used to kill pests such as insects.

photosynthesis: the process plants use to turn sunlight, carbon dioxide, and water into food.

phytoplankton: tiny, drifting plants, such as algae, that live in both salt water and fresh water.

polar ice cap: a dome-shaped sheet of ice found at both the North and South Poles.

polar ice sheet: one of several sheets of ice found in the Arctic and Antarctica.

pollution: waste that harms the environment.

precipitation: the falling to the earth of rain, snow, or any form of water.

predator: an animal that preys on others.

prey: an animal caught or hunted for food.

primary consumers: organisms that eat plants.

producer: an organism that makes its own food, usually from sunlight, air, water, and soil.

R

reptile: an animal covered with scales that moves on its belly or on short legs. It changes its body temperature by moving to warmer or cooler places. Snakes, turtles, and alligators are reptiles.

roost: a place where birds settle to rest.

runoff: the water from precipitation that drains or flows over the ground into a body of water or a wetland.

S

salinity: the salt content of water or soil.

saturated: full of water.

sea level: the level of the surface of the sea.

secondary consumers: organisms that eat primary consumers.

sedge: a grass-like plant. Many different sedges grow in wetlands.

sediment: bits of rock, sand, or dirt that have been carried to a place by water, wind, or a glacier.

soil: the top layer of the earth, in which plants grow.

spawn: to produce and deposit eggs.

species: a group of living things that are closely related and can produce young.

specimen: a sample used for study.

submerged plant: a plant that lives entirely underwater.

swamp: an area of wet ground that grows woody plants such as trees and shrubs.

T

terrestrial: relating to the earth or non-saturated soil.

thermal expansion: the ways matter changes in response to a change in temperature.

tide: the twice daily rising and falling of ocean water.

V

vegetation: all the plant life in a particular area.

vernal pool: a temporary body of water that forms from rainwater or snowmelt in the spring or the fall. Vernal pools provide plant and animal habitats, but fish don't live here.

vulnerable: exposed to harm.

W

waste stream: the flow of waste from a home, business or industrial area to its final destination.

waterway: a channel or body of water.

wetland: land that is soaked with water for part of the year, such as a marsh or swamp.

Z

zooplankton: tiny animals that drift freely in salt water and fresh water.

METRIC CONVERSIONS

Use this chart to find the metric equivalents to the English measurements in this book. If you need to know a half measurement, divide by two. If you need to know twice the measurement, multiply by two. How do you find a quarter measurement? How do you find three times the measurement?

English	Metric
1 inch	2.5 centimeters
1 foot	30.5 centimeters
1 yard	0.9 meter
1 mile	1.6 kilometers
1 pound	0.5 kilogram
1 teaspoon	5 milliliters
1 tablespoon	15 milliliters
1 cup	237 milliliters

BOOKS

Aquatic Wild: K-12 Curriculum and Activity Guide (Project Wild, Council for Environmental Education, 2016)

Yasuda, Anita. *Explore Water! With 25 Great Projects, Activities, and Experiments*. Nomad, 2011

Mooney, Carla. *Explore Rivers and Ponds! With 25 Great Projects*. Nomad, 2012

Johansson, Philip. *Marshes and Swamps: A Wetland Web of Life*. Enslow, 2007

Kurtz, Kevin. *A Day in the Salt Marsh*. Sylvan Dell, 2007

Aloian, Molly, and Bobbie Kalman. *A Wetland Habitat*. Crabtree Publications, 2006

Kalman, Bobbie. *What are Wetlands?* Crabtree Publications, 2002

WEBSITES

Cornell Lab of Ornithology
allaboutbirds.org/mesmerizing-migration-watch-118-bird-species-migrate-across-a-map-of-the-western-hemisphere

Council for Environmental Education
councilforee.org

Defenders of Wildlife
defenders.org

Ducks Unlimited
ducks.org

Earth Echo (World Water Monitoring Day)
worldwatermonitoringday.org

Earth Island Institute
earthisland.org

The Groundwater Foundation
groundwater.org

Izaak Walton League of America
iwla.org

NASA
Project Science, Global Monitoring of Wetland and Extent Dynamics
wetlands.jpl.nasa.gov

National Audubon Society
aududobon.org

National Environmental Education Fund
neefusa.org

National Geographic Society
nationalgeographic.com

National Oceanic and Atmospheric Administration National Ocean Service
oceanservice.noaa.gov/facts/wetland.html

National Park Service
nps.gov

National Water Quality Monitoring Council
acwi.gov/monitoring/vm

National Wildlife Federation
nwf.org

The Nature Conservancy
nature.org

Project Wild
projectwild.org

U.S. Environmental Protection Agency Wetlands Protection and Restoration
epa.gov/wetlands

USDA Natural Resources Conservation Service
nrcs.usda.gov

U.S. Fish and Wildlife Service National Wetlands Inventory
fws.gov/wetlands

World Wetlands Day
worldwetlandsday.org

World Wildlife Fund Wetland habitats
worldwildlife.org/habitats/wetlands

QR CODE GLOSSARY

Page 8: youtube.com/watch?v=aladpRIVdRI

Page 17: worldwetlandsday.org

Page 27: nature.org/ourinitiatives/regions/northamerica/
unitedstates/florida/placesweprotect/everglades.xml

Page 34: youtube.com/watch?v=zN8QN-g7kjY

Page 48: nationalgeographic.com/magazine/2018/03/
bird-migration-interactive-maps/

Page 50: fisheries.noaa.gov/welcome

Page 61: ispotnature.org/communities/uk-and-ireland

Page 63: earthobservatory.nasa.gov/Features/WorldOfChange/decadaltemp.php

Page 65: nbcnews.com/news/weather/video/
boston-hit-by-coastal-flooding-in-massive-winter-storm-1129382467616

Page 66: usgs.gov/products/maps/overview

Page 77: wikiwatershed.org

Page 79: water.usgs.gov/edu/waterquality.html

ESSENTIAL QUESTIONS

Introduction: What is the difference between a marsh and a swamp?

Chapter 1: What role do wetlands play in our environment?

Chapter 2: In what ways are plants an important part of a wetland?

Chapter 3: Why is it important to have both predators
and prey living in an ecosystem?

Chapter 4: How might climate change affect the area you live in?

Chapter 5: What can you do to help keep wetlands healthy in your town?